MAPPING A WINNING TRAINING APPROACH

A Practical Guide To Choosing The Right Training Methods

Joe B. Wilson

Jossey-Bass
Pfeiffer
San Francisco

RICHARD
CHANG
ASSOCIATES

ISBN: 0-7879-5099-8

Published by

350 Sansome Street, 5th Floor
San Francisco, California 94104-1342
(415) 433-1740; Fax (415) 433-0499
(800) 274-4434; Fax (800) 569-0443

www.pfeiffer.com

Printing   10   9   8   7   6   5   4   3   2   1

ACKNOWLEDGMENTS

About The Author

Joe Wilson, a Vice President of Richard Chang Associates, Inc., is a training consultant and instructional media producer with more than 20 years of international experience. He has a broad background in the development of video, print, and computer-based instructional programs—from needs analysis through design, production, implementation, and evaluation. His experience in project management, development, and delivery of training programs spans a wide range—from highly technical systems projects, to management/sales development, to Total Quality implementations.

The author would like to acknowledge the support of the entire team of professionals at Richard Chang Associates, Inc. for their contribution to the guidebook development process. In addition, special thanks are extended to the many client organizations who have helped us shape the practical ideas and proven methods shared in this guidebook.

Additional Credits

Editor: Sarah Ortlieb Fraser

Reviewers: Ruth Stingley and Pamela Wade

Graphic Layout: Dottie Snyder

Cover Design: John Odam Design Associates

PREFACE

The 1990's have already presented individuals and organizations with some very difficult challenges to face and overcome. So who will have the advantage as we move toward the year 2000 and beyond?

The advantage will belong to those with a commitment to continuous learning. Whether on an individual basis or as an entire organization, one key ingredient to building a continuous learning environment is *The Practical Guidebook Collection* brought to you by the Publications Division of Richard Chang Associates, Inc.

After understanding the future *"learning needs"* expressed by our clients and other potential customers, we are pleased to publish *The Practical Guidebook Collection*. These guidebooks are designed to provide you with proven, *"real-world"* tips, tools, and techniques—on a wide range of subjects—that you can apply in the workplace and/or on a personal level immediately.

Once you've had a chance to benefit from *The Practical Guidebook Collection*, please share your feedback with us. We've included a brief *Evaluation and Feedback Form* at the end of the guidebook that you can fax to us at (714) 756-0853.

With your feedback, we can continuously improve the resources we are providing through the Publications Division of Richard Chang Associates, Inc.

Wishing you successful reading,

[signature]

Richard Y. Chang
President and CEO
Richard Chang Associates, Inc.

TABLE OF CONTENTS

> *"Would you tell me please, which way I ought to go from here?"*
>
> *"That depends a good deal on where you want to get to,"*
>
> *"I don't much care where"*
>
> *"Then it doesn't matter which way you go"*
>
> Lewis Carroll

CHAPTER ONE

INTRODUCTION

Why Read This Guidebook?

Training can be risky. You might spend thousands of dollars and invest eons of hours, only to discover that your organization's productivity hasn't improved. That fear could be the reason why you've opened this guidebook. Your job is on the line. You want your training efforts to succeed.

You *can* eliminate much of the risk. If, that is, you invest in learning how to make your training efforts impact your organization in a positive manner. Gone are the days when you could just slap together a training program and everyone was happy if it seemed to work. Successful training requires a knowledge of what works and a plan for applying that knowledge effectively.

Organizations today don't want training that *might* work. They want training that *does* work. And training that works does take some effort. However, the payoff on your investment more than makes up for the hours and dollars spent in preparation, implementation, measurement, and follow-through.

Your time will be invested wisely by using this guidebook. It'll guide you toward success. Mapping your training approach is a critical element in planning for great training. If you follow the tips in this guidebook, you'll stay focused on your results. And that's what's needed if your training is to accomplish anything worthwhile.

Those who don't map their training approaches end up slinging quarters into the slot machine of improbable success. Their likelihood of a great payoff? Very slim. So read on to carefully design your training effort.

Who Should Read This Guidebook?

Chances are, most people in an organization could use this guidebook. That's because the odds are that most employees will be asked at some point in their careers to train another individual or group. Whether you are a manager, supervisor, team leader, or even an experienced trainer, you could benefit from reading this guidebook.

MAP YOUR TRAINING APPROACH

You wouldn't have picked up *Mapping A Winning Training Approach* unless you were interested in making a current or future training effort successful. If you've trained before, but chose the quickest or easiest way to handle the situation, you might be interested in learning how to systematically choose a winning approach. Perhaps the idea that there is more than one training approach strikes you as a novel one. Read on.

Maybe you've moved up in your organization. Your new job description involves quite a bit of training and you want your first review to be glowing. Remember that training doesn't come naturally. It's honed through practice.

Even if you're secure in your abilities as a trainer, consider improving your training efforts. Have you ever trained a group and later discovered that the individuals in that group needed retraining? Maybe a refresher course in planning your training effort would prove insightful. *Mapping A Winning Training Approach* puts you on the right track.

When And How To Use It

Since training is an investment, your payoff will be greater the sooner you start and the more you invest. So read through this guidebook carefully. Once you've identified your training needs, you can concentrate on preparing for the training. If you take your time to prepare well, the rewards will multiply.

If you're already in the midst of training, pause and read through this guidebook. You may find that it is beneficial to restructure your training approach to fit the needs of your trainees. Or you might discover that you need additional training to meet performance goals you never set. It's not too late to change your investment strategy.

What if you've just finished training? You can identify where your training should have taken you and what methods might have been better. If you didn't reach your goals, learn how you can. You'll probably have another opportunity to train, and now you'll know how to invest your energy to reap dividends!

IDENTIFY YOUR TRAINING NEEDS

Mapping your training approach isn't the first item of business in developing training that works. Identifying your training needs takes precedence. It's the first phase of the High-IMPACT Training™ Model, and it sets the stage for any successful training effort.

The High-IMPACT Training™ Model

The High-IMPACT Training™ Model is a six-phase process designed to provide effective, targeted training. Follow this model to invest wisely in your training.

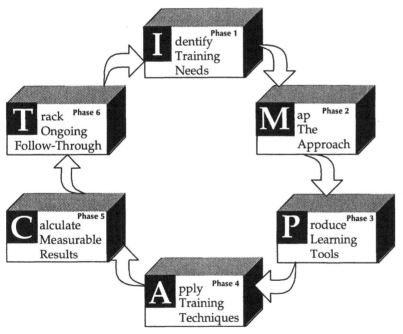

The High-IMPACT Training™ Model

Each completed phase of the High-IMPACT Training Model adds value to your investment. The table on the next page illustrates what occurs during each of the six phases.

PHASE	DESCRIPTION
1. **I** dentify **Training Needs**	Determine if and how training can play a role in improving job performance; target training outcomes.
2. **M** ap The Approach	Choose the appropriate training approach(es) that will best support the targeted outcomes and improve job performance.
3. **P** roduce Learning **Tools**	Produce all training/coaching components (*e.g., materials, audiovisual aids, job aids,* etc.).
4. **A** pply Training **Techniques**	Deliver the training as designed to ensure successful results.
5. **C** alculate **Measurable Results**	Assess whether your training/coaching accomplished actual performance improvement, communicate the results, and redesign the process as necessary.
6. **T** rack Ongoing **Follow-Through**	Hone in on the techniques that individuals and organizations can use to ensure that the impact of their training does not diminish.

Mapping A Winning Training Approach briefly discusses Phase One and fully details Phase Two of the High-IMPACT Training Model. It will prepare you for successful training.

Conducting A Needs Analysis

TRAINING NEEDS

Understanding your training needs is the first step on the path to effective training. In the first phase of the High-IMPACT Training Model, you'll undertake a needs analysis to ensure that the training you do addresses your particular situation. It is both costly and embarrassing to recommend a direction that has no impact on the issue at hand. When you do a needs analysis, you focus your attention on the target and identify the means for getting there. You also involve others in the process and help them understand the issues you are all facing.

To complete a needs analysis, follow these six steps:

- Assess your current situation
- Envision your future
- Gather information
- Sort your information
- Share your results
- Decide your next step

Assess your current situation

In a needs analysis, assessing your current situation enables you to clearly define your problem. All of your other actions in the needs analysis depend on the accuracy of your initial assessment. It's a critical first step.

To view the complete picture of your current situation, ask yourself the following three questions:

Where are we now?
Explore the current situation; start by noting what you already know about your situation in measurable terms. Have sales dropped? Is manufacturing behind in production? Is customer satisfaction where it should be? Ask others in the organization to help you assess the situation.

Why do we think we need training?
Go beyond the obvious. Think carefully about the situation. Is there a history for this situation? What is the issue, problem, or situation that is creating the need or demand for training? And will training effectively meet the need?

What organizational issues are driving the need for training?
Look at the larger picture that should be a part of your overall strategy. If you know what the mission, vision, and business objectives of your organization are, you should be able to determine what is going on in your organization that is driving the need for training.

Envision your future

Envisioning your future involves defining and understanding what training will accomplish. When you think about how the future will look if your training efforts are successful, you often discover aspects of your vision that have nothing to do with training, but are critical to the success of your efforts. If you uncover these elements early in your needs analysis, you can address them as well.

To create your vision, ask yourself these three questions:

1. Where do we want to be?

You've already assessed your current situation. Now you must develop an equally careful description of the future, again in measurable terms. Use your imagination to see your trainees as they would be if the issues of the current situation were successfully addressed. Maybe customer service representatives will be more knowledgeable, or perhaps the shipping department will be able to handle orders more productively.

2. What would success look like?

How would things be different if the issues were resolved successfully? Think about how the solution would help your external customers and your entire organization. What measurable benefits would result if your dream of the future came true?

3. Do we have the whole picture?

Your vision of the future must also consider the complete needs of others. Would your solution benefit the organization as a whole? Will it benefit your customers in their most critical areas?

It can't be stressed enough that you must use quantifiable measures and data to indicate success. These numbers are an important component to your training plan, so include them in your description of the future.

INCREASED SALES

DECREASED ERRORS

REDUCED NUMBER OF RETURNS

REDUCED CYCLE TIME

INCREASED MORALE

DECREASED CUSTOMER COMPLAINTS

Enlarging the picture also reveals key players outside your group of trainees whose involvement may be essential to the success of your needs analysis. By identifying others who have a stake in the success of your project, you expand your resources and increase your chances of success.

Gather information

The information-gathering step is an opportunity for you to collect raw data from whatever sources you feel would be helpful. You are investigating to discover:

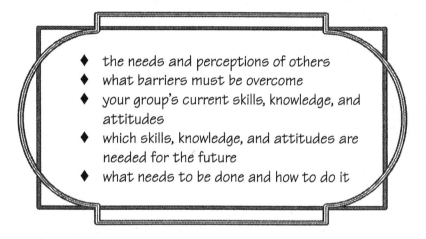

- the needs and perceptions of others
- what barriers must be overcome
- your group's current skills, knowledge, and attitudes
- which skills, knowledge, and attitudes are needed for the future
- what needs to be done and how to do it

Whom should you ask?
Ask individuals who know the most about the situation, those who want to be involved, and those who would be critical to the success of the project. In addition, consider asking those who might have a different perspective or who can provide objective information.

What should you ask?

Explain to participants the purpose of the needs analysis and share with them the desired future state. Don't be surprised if they want to add details to the future-state description. You are the best judge of what questions you should ask, but here are a few suggestions:

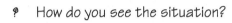

- ? How do you see the situation?

- ? What do you think needs to be done?

- ? What, if any, training is needed?

- ? Specifically, how would that training help?

- ? What concerns do you have about improving the situation?

- ? Is there anyone else you think we should talk to?

How should you ask?

Using a variety of methods is usually best. One example of this would be using interviews for management, surveys and questionnaires with employees, and focus groups with customers—all in the same needs analysis. It really doesn't matter how many methods you employ; concentrate on getting the information you need in an appropriate, timely, and courteous manner.

Sort your information

 What should you do with all the information you've gathered? You need to sort it into categories to help you manage it and to identify themes and issues that must be addressed to reach your vision of the future.

When you sort your information into categories, you are looking for consistencies and connections between individual pieces of information. Once you've categorized your information and looked at the significance of each contribution, you can begin to prioritize the issues. How you do this depends on your specific situation.

You might want to start with the category with the most comments, or you might want to start with the positive categories and then list the negative ones. Depending upon your situation, it might be best to address the organizational themes first and then the team themes or individual needs.

Share your results

When you share your results with others, your goal is to present the information in a way that will move you forward. Offer hope for solutions to address needs and be prepared with recommendations to share as well.

What to share is the challenging part, but *how* to share it is also an important consideration. Be positive and encouraging. Use every opportunity to provide measures and facts to back up your recommendations.

Consider using visuals or charts to support your information. It gives those present another way to interpret what you're saying. Examples and metaphors can also help your audience understand the material. Be sure to have the raw data available as backup. Someone might ask to see it.

Decide your next step

The last action in the needs-analysis process is to translate the recommendations into a plan of action. You will create a list of activities that will be used in the next phases. There are three key elements to a successful action plan:

Determining the actions needed

If your recommendations are not currently worded as specific actions, rewrite them so they are.

Distributing responsibilities

Each action in your action plan should be assigned to a specific person to do, within a defined budget. Better yet, ask for volunteers. If a team will be performing the task, record the name of one person on the team as the lead contact.

Establishing a time line

For each action item, establish a due date for completion of the task. This will give participants a target to aim at and help them focus their activities toward results.

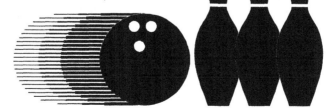

A Four-Step Mapping Process

Once you've identified your targeted training needs, you're ready to chart your course through an instructional mapping process.

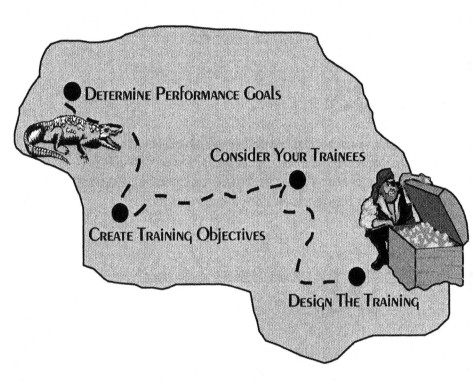

Read on to learn how each of these steps will lead you to a successful training plan.

CHAPTER TWO WORKSHEET:
CONDUCTING YOUR NEEDS ANALYSIS

1. Consider a current work situation in which training might improve performance. Why do you think training would be efffective, as opposed to improving compensation, work tools, work space, etc.?

_____

_____

_____

_____

_____

_____

_____

_____

_____

_____

_____

_____

_____

_____

_____

2. Describe what you think the training will accomplish.

_____

_____

_____

_____

_____

_____

_____

_____

_____

_____

_____

_____

_____

_____

_____

_____

_____

_____

3. List the people who will be affected by the training.

_____

_____

_____

_____

_____

_____

_____

4. Describe your next step.

_____

_____

_____

_____

_____

_____

_____

DETERMINE PERFORMANCE GOALS

A needs analysis provides a firm foundation on which you can build your training effort. It gives you ideas and suggestions that you can research further. And you've already taken an initial look at how performance can be improved.

Here's where performance goals come in. All training is aimed at improving performance, whether it involves teaching employees *knowledge* they don't currently have, *skills* they have yet to master, and/or motivating them to change their *attitudes*. If you can't improve performance, training may prove to be a waste of time and money. Performance goals based on systematic research provide a clear direction for training.

KNOWLEDGE

SKILLS

ATTITUDE

Link Performance Goals To Organizational Goals

Choose your performance goals with organizational goals in mind. Does this sound too obvious? It may, but you'd be surprised at how often the two aren't linked. Some organizations spend thousands of dollars upgrading computer systems when the money spent doesn't translate into increased profitability, a common organizational goal *(at least in the private sector!)* The money might be better spent on teaching customer service representatives about products *(knowledge)*, training warehouse personnel on shipping techniques *(skills)*, or motivating sales reps to be excited about a new product *(attitudes)*.

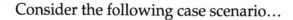

Consider the following case scenario…

Country Kitchens, a statewide fast-food chain …

added *"linguine with clam sauce"* to its menu after conducting market research. The research indicated that by adding gourmet food to their menu, they would draw in customers that may not usually go to a *"fast-food"* restaurant. Nigel Christensen, owner and CEO, made sure that only the best ingredients went into his sauce, and that the pasta was made fresh on the premises of each restaurant. Because Country Kitchens is a fast-food restaurant, the linguine must be prepared quickly and inexpensively, and yet be flavorful.

Initially, the linguine was in high demand, thanks to a heavily aired television commercial, but word started to spread that the dish wasn't very good. Since Country Kitchens remained dedicated to the linguine, they saw a potential fiasco on their hands. They vowed to spend whatever it took to rectify the problem. In search of a solution, Nigel hired an outside consultant, Merilynne Gurney, to research the problem.

Nigel explained to Merilynne that she needed to discover why the dish wasn't selling. *"We've invested a lot of money on 'easy-to-use' high-tech pasta machines,"* he said. *"So we stand to lose money on the machines, and we'll more than likely lose customers if our reputation suffers."*

Merilynne began by conducting a needs analysis. She visited several of the fast-food restaurants and gathered information. She discovered that the employees, mostly part-time high school and college students, were having a hard time making the linguine. It either came out *"gooey"* or dry, in spite of the fact that Country Kitchens purchased expensive machines. Further investigation revealed that the installation and usage kit that was distributed to every restaurant included a confusing instruction booklet that was similar to a comic book—all illustrations and hardly any text—apparently in an attempt to bridge cultural and language barriers. Several managers told her that arguments erupted over the various interpretations employees gathered from the booklet.

Merilynne reported back to Nigel. *"We now know that the problem isn't freshness of ingredients or timeliness of delivery. In fact,"* she added, *"I think we've isolated the problem. It has to do with the texture of the linguine. It's not consistent, and neither is the way the employees operate the machines."* She paused for a moment. *"When the linguine is properly prepared, customers like the product."* *"What do we need to do?"* Nigel asked. *"My initial guess is that we need to train the employees to operate the machines correctly,"* Merilynne countered. *"And I'm going to look into that approach more closely this week."*…

Clearly you'll want to make sure that you're focused on what your organization deems important, and set performance goals that are linked to corporate goals. Usually, this means that you'll also need to take a close look at customer expectations, since most organizations' goals are related to and/or affected by customer expectations. You'll analyze output and in-process measures. Put in layperson's terms, you will check to see that both what you're making *(output)* and how you're doing it *(in-process tasks)* meet customer expectations.

Maybe the widgets you manufacture could be bigger or better. Or perhaps the widgets are fantastic, but they take too long to make. If your customers aren't satisfied, find out why. Don't waste time training if it's not going to ultimately make a difference to your customers. Training must address concerns that affect the bottom line, which is directly related to customer satisfaction and retention.

Create Descriptive Performance Goals

Once you've uncovered where you think training is needed to improve performance, and you've discovered that a performance improvement in that area will be in line with corporate goals, you need to scrutinize the performance that must be improved. Your research isn't over; it has just begun.

Job descriptions

Many organizations don't have written job descriptions for their employees. If a written job description for your potential trainees doesn't exist, write one and include how you expect the employees to perform in measurable terms. If current job descriptions don't include your performance expectations, rewrite the job descriptions. Add how employees should perform their tasks *(in-process work)* and what the result should look like *(the output)*.

Performance checks

Take a good look at your potential trainees, and schedule *"performance checks"* to observe them in action. How close are they to fulfilling your output and/or in-process measures? Analyzing their performance before you design training will help you set descriptive performance goals.

In your performance checks, you'll be concentrating closely on what your potential trainees *are* doing and what they *aren't (but should be)* doing. The difference between what they are doing *(current performance)* and what they should be doing *(performance goal)* is a performance gap. If the gap is minuscule, a full-fledged training effort may not be warranted. If the gap is a huge canyon, identify specific areas of concern and focus on them.

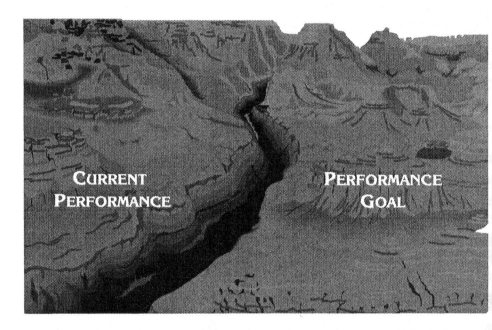

Performance checks are a wise investment of your time. Why? Because they enable you to validate the descriptive performance goals included in the job description.

Using performance goals

Your performance goals, then, will become expected performances for any new employees, and will automatically be taken into account for all employees during review time. This makes for good training. You'll train employees to achieve goals for which they'll ultimately be held accountable.

This goal will be more attainable, because:

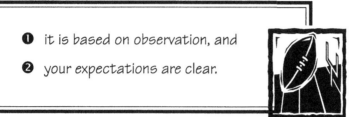

❶ it is based on observation, and

❷ your expectations are clear.

Training, then, can focus on ensuring that this particular goal will be achieved back on the job. Vague expectations result in vague and inconsistent performance. Clear and achievable expectations set the stage for targeted training and improved performance back on the job.

Let's say it's taking too long to process orders in your organization. You decide that a performance goal for order-entry clerks is to enter orders more quickly. Will training help them reach that goal? Perhaps. But your expectations for improvement are so vague that success will be difficult to measure.

On the other hand, you might strategically conduct performance checks and carefully observe the order-entry clerks as they process orders. You could then add to their job description a descriptive, measurable performance goal such as *"process an average of twenty orders per hour (one every three minutes)."*

Performance checks also allow you to determine if you're targeting the right trainees. Maybe the order entry clerks can't process orders faster than they presently are doing because the sales representatives aren't filling out all the information on the order forms and the clerks have to call customers to obtain missing information.

You've discovered in your performance checks that the order-entry clerks can't process the orders more quickly because of issues that don't relate to their training. Whoops! You've got the wrong group of trainees. *(Better to discover it now than after pouring time and money into training that doesn't have a chance of improving performance!)*

NOW VIEWING

Merilynne revisited ...

several of Country Kitchens' locations and observed the employees making the linguine. In addition, she carefully read the instruction booklet. *"It definitely could use a revision,"* she commented to one manager. *"I'll say,"* was his reply.

But the instruction booklet wasn't the only glitch in the process. Merilynne suspected that something was blocking the motivation of store management and employees.

Nevertheless, considering the performance checks she conducted, Merilynne did decide that training could possibly help employees learn to make linguine correctly every single time, *"But first I'd like to meet with some of the company's managers to solicit their input,"* she informed Nigel. *"Then I'll write a job description for employees that includes processes and measures for the output we want—excellent linguine with clam sauce."*

Determine Measurable Performance Goals

If you set performance goals that are measurable, you're way ahead of the game. Many trainers feel that improvement is important, and as long as they see some gains, they feel they've succeeded. But how can you truly determine the success of your training effort unless you can measure it?

Initial measurements

Your performance checks will provide you with the initial current measurements. For example, if the order-entry clerks you read about earlier are currently processing an average of ten orders per hour, and your performance goal is set at twenty, you're anticipating that training will increase their performance by one hundred percent. If they process fifteen orders an hour after training has ended, they've upped their performance by fifty percent and are halfway toward their goal. Maybe in two months, they'll be processing nineteen orders every hour, and in three months, they'll reach twenty-one. You'll have exceeded your goal!

If your performance goals are measurable, and they meet both internal and external customer expectations, you can prove the worth of your training. Additionally, you give your trainees something to shoot for. A descriptive, measurable goal is a valuable asset. It allows you to develop accurate training objectives, which are described in the following chapter.

So determine your performance goals. Make sure they're linked to corporate goals and written measurable job descriptions. Conduct performance checks to validate performance expectations. In short, successful training demands solid research, a necessary component of any good investment.

CHAPTER THREE WORKSHEET:
DETERMINE PERFORMANCE GOALS

1. List the strategic goals of your organization. Next consider a specific training effort you're involved with now. Write check marks next to the goals to which your training effort is closely linked.

---

2. Write down three measurable *"in-process"* performance goals for processes used in your organization.

_____

_____

_____

_____

_____

_____

3. Write down three measurable *"output"* goals for products or services your organization provides.

_____

_____

_____

_____

_____

_____

CREATE TRAINING OBJECTIVES

The descriptive, measurable performance goals you set in the previous chapter are in place. But can training help you reach these goals? Don't skip this chapter. You'll learn how to answer the question above and learn how to write training objectives that support your performance goals. Trainers who don't create training objectives are like rebels without a cause. Their efforts are bound to be misplaced.

Determine If Training Will Help

Let's say your potential trainees have to bridge a performance gap to improve their performance and reach your expectations.

You're banking on the possibility that training will help them vault over the canyon. But will it really? Don't wait until after training takes place to determine its value. Figure it out now. Your performance checks and the information you gathered in your needs analysis should provide you with a good background for your investigative work.

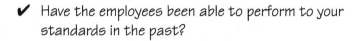
Ask yourself the following questions:

- ✔ Have the employees been able to perform to your standards in the past?

- ✔ If they have, will retraining help them?
  (Or will additional practice be sufficient to improve performance?)

- ✔ If they haven't performed adequately in the past, will training help them or can you bypass training by simplifying the job or providing job aids?

- ✔ Can you bypass training by changing elements about the job to help employees perform to your expectations *(e.g., provide additional compensation, better work tools, change the work environment or culture, improve work policies and procedures, etc.)?*

- ✔ Are employees motivated to perform to your standards?

- ✔ Are employees penalized for not performing to your standards?

You have to determine *why* a performance gap exists. Can the deficiency be tied to a lack of knowledge or skills? Is it a lack of motivation on the part of the employees? Or can it be attributed to external factors such as pay or environment? Training is a plausible solution *only* if you can improve performance by increasing employees' knowledge or skills or by changing their attitudes. If employees aren't performing up to your new standards because they're dissatisfied with their pay, they can't concentrate in a noisy environment, or their computer equipment is antiquated and keeps breaking down, your training will have little or no impact.

Merilynne met with the general managers

from a variety of Country Kitchens locations. *"I think training will help your employees learn how to make linguine that comes out perfectly, but I need your input, too,"* she began. *"What are your opinions? Do your employees know how to operate the pasta machines, but just aren't doing what they've been told?"*

One of the managers, Lionel, spoke up. *"They really don't know how to operate the machines very well. I'm not even sure we know how to do it. Everyone has a different idea, and the instruction book is no help."* Murmurs of agreement came from the rest of the managers. Lionel continued, *"Unless the machines aren't working properly, I think training will help. Something better help. We're just tired of the added confusion."*

Other managers seconded Lionel's statement. The more they talked about the disruption, the more Merilynne discovered that they weren't happy with the addition of linguine to the menu. *"We have enough to worry about with burgers,"* one added. *"Now we just have more work for the same pay."*

"You mean less pay," another manager interjected. *"The linguine fiasco is eating into our profits. Our bonuses this year are looking worse all the time." Frankly, morale is pretty low in our restaurant."*

"Why don't I discuss the issue with Nigel," Merilynne offered. *You can't train your employees successfully if you're not happy with the whole linguine business."*

Nigel was interested in Merilynne's observations. *"I guess it makes sense,"* he said. *"I was sure the linguine would raise profits for Country Kitchens, and the managers would get their share."* As the two talked it out, Nigel decided to increase manager bonus incentives based on profits from linguine sales. *"Do you think that will motivate for the managers to make the linguine a success?"* He asked. *"Yes,"* Merilynne responded. *"Now you've got the managers covered. But we still have to train the employees."*...

f you can determine that training will help, **h**en continue with the High-IMPACT Training **M**odel. If your research causes you to doubt that **t** will, you may be led to another endeavor, **s**uch as revising a work process, modifying **t**he work environment, or purchasing **n**ew work tools.

Consider Knowledge, Skills, And Attitude

If you have concluded that training will help employees bridge the performance gap, you'll want to keep in mind the three basic types of training:

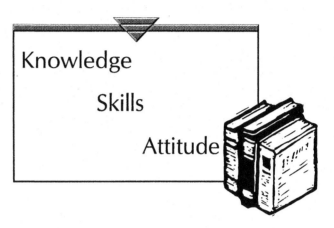

Knowledge

Skills

Attitude

Are your employees not performing well because they need more information to perform the duties you require? Your training should strive to increase your trainees' knowledge. Are their skills deficient? Your training must ensure that their skill levels improve. If your trainees need to develop different attitudes, your training should focus on that area.

Why focus on the three types of training at this point? Because if you don't, your training won't be targeted to the needs of your trainees and the requirements of your organization. You may try to teach them skills they've already mastered, when it's their attitudes that are blocking expected performance. Or, you may make the mistake of pumping them full of information they already know, which will waste everyone's time. When you finally attempt to adjust their attitudes, they'll have tuned you out!

Merilynne set up another meeting ...

with the general managers. *"The good news,"* she began, *"is that your efforts will be rewarded. And the machines work fine. Our challenge, then, is to develop appropriate training to teach the employees the correct way to make*  linguine the customers will like.*"* One of the managers, Diane, held up her hand. *"Can that really be done?"* She asked. *"I believe so,"* Merilynne replied. *"It'll require a combination of knowledge, skills, and attitude. We're not talking about flipping burgers here. Making linguine with clam sauce is more intricate. We have to transform the burger cooks into chefs. They need to know the correct combinations and measurements of the ingredients and the timing involved. They need to learn how to operate the machine correctly, and they need to improve their attitudes. I'd like to ask a couple of you to volunteer to work with me on developing objectives and designing an approach that is geared toward your employees. Any takers?"*

Diane and Lionel agreed to assist Merilynne with the project ahead of her. ...

Create Training Objectives

You've decided that training is the best way to bridge the performance gap, and you've decided whether your trainees need training in the area(s) of attitude, skills, or knowledge. To get the best possible results from your training effort, you need to create training objectives. But why? You can't choose your training

approach and prepare your materials if you don't know what you want to accomplish. In the same vein, architects can't begin to design a house unless they know the homeowner's requirements. In turn, interior decorators don't choose materials, furniture, and accessories until they know what effects their clients are trying to achieve.

In addition, training objectives provide a checkpoint. You can test your trainees to see if they can perform at the expected level in a risk-free training environment. Within this realm, your employees have a chance to practice and demonstrate skills without jeopardizing customer expectations for quality.

Creating training objectives is a simple way to keep you focused on the expected end results of your training. Training objectives are nothing more than statements about what performances you want your trainees to display after training has ended.

Before

After

In basic terms, you should think about: What will my trainees be able to do after training, and how well must they do it?

Training objectives always state what the trainees will be doing in measurable terms. In other words, the objectives include some kind of performance expectation. If your objectives don't, rewrite them so they do. Your understanding and your employees' understanding of exactly how things are to be done and what the final product is supposed to look like must be the same. So write specific, measurable training objectives. Don't leave your objectives open to interpretation.

Here are a few examples of both good and poor objectives.

Good

- ○ Trainees will verbally describe four dangers of improperly handled toxic waste.

- ○ Using all the keys, trainees will be able to type 60 wpm on the computer.

- ○ Trainees will be able to recite the procedure of handling a cash transaction.

- ○ Trainees will perform all five steps involved in keying in an order, in the correct order, and within four minutes.

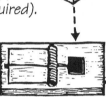

Poor

 Trainees understand the danger of toxic waste.
(Not specific enough. No performance is required).

 Trainees will improve their typing.
(Not specific enough).

 Trainees practice handling a cash transaction.
(No performance is required).

 Trainees develop a knowledge of order entry.
(Not specific enough. No performance is required).

Merilynne, Lionel, and Diane met ...

to work on the training objectives for the employees at Country Kitchens.

First, they made a rough list of desired knowledge, skills and attitudes. In order to make perfect linguine, they need to be able to use the pasta machine, make the dough, and cook the sauce. Before employees can learn the skills of using the pasta machine they need to understand the directions. Before learning to make dough, employees need to know how to read a recipe.

Advanced knowledge, skills and attitude

To read a sauce recipe, employees need to decode abbreviations. And the knowledge and skills have to be handled with a more professional demeanor—a *"chef's"* attitude.

Next, they constructed a list of objectives representing the skills, items of knowledge, and desired attitudes each employee needed to master and/or demonstrate to make linguine perfectly.

Basic knowledge, skills and attitude

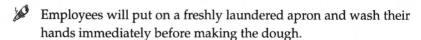

Some of the objectives were:

- 📣 Employees will put on a freshly laundered apron and wash their hands immediately before making the dough.

- 📣 Given measuring cups and spoons, employees will be able to measure each ingredient correctly 100% of the time.

- 📣 Employees will be able to read the recipe, including all abbreviations.

- 📣 Employees will demonstrate each recipe step in order, taking no more than one minute on each step.

- 📣 Employees will mix the dough by hand for three minutes.

- 📣 Employees will be able to explain the importance of completing all steps accurately and completely.

Writing Training Objectives Related To Attitudes

If your training effort involves primarily attitude improvement, you're probably fidgeting in your seat. You might be saying, *"how am I supposed to teach and measure attitude improvement?"*

Admittedly, it's not as easy to formulate training objectives for attitude adjusting, but it can be done. How do you write training objectives for trainees you'd like to become more professional, motivated, careful, or positive? You need to think carefully about what attitudes you want to see demonstrated.

Then start to brainstorm the performances that come to mind. Don't worry about how crazy they appear. You'll weed out the unacceptable responses after you're finished. Keep writing until you can't think of any more desired behaviors.

For example, you may include in your list:

answers phone courteously

works late every day

finishes projects on time

smiles often

offers help to others

dresses appropriately

works well independently

works well in a group

keeps work area organized

supports teamwork

demonstrates commitment

When you're done with your list, expand on each item by trying to write a sentence about it. For example, if you want to train your employees to be more professional, and one item on your list is "dress appropriately," you might end up with:

❶ Employees will wear suits at all times.
(Or)
❷ Male employees will wear dark suits
and dress shoes,
and
female employees will wear blouses,
knee-length skirts or professional slacks,
and dress shoes.

Continue until you have a list of acceptable behaviors or attitudes.

Next, you'll have to determine which items on your list trainees already follow; those that remain are the ones you will cover in your training effort for current employees. For new trainees, you will cover all items on your list. When your trainees consistently demonstrate the attitudes you have identified, they will have met your performance expectations.

Determining the necessity of training and creating training objectives help build success into the training process. And if you keep the objectives at the forefront of your planning, you'll stay focused on eliminating the identified performance gaps. It's critical to your training investment strategy!

Training Objectives

CHAPTER FOUR WORKSHEET:
CREATE TRAINING OBJECTIVES

. List two good training objectives for *"knowledge"* performance expectations.

_____

_____

_____

_____

2. List two good training objectives for *"skills"* performance expectations.

_____

_____

_____

_____

3. List two good training objectives for *"attitude"* performance expectations.

_____

_____

_____

_____

CONSIDER YOUR TRAINEES

Consider training as a vehicle that has to pick up your trainees and *move* them from inadequate to required performance. Can it be done? You bet—but not without carefully considering your trainees.

"Move" is the operative word here. You might want to substitute it with prod, push, motivate, empower, spur, or goad, but the concept remains the same! Somehow you have to get your trainees from point A *(what they presently are doing, what they already know, or how they currently are acting)* to point B *(what they need to be doing, what they must know, or how they need to be acting).*

One group of trainees might need only a brief, large-group lecture in a classroom, a few practice exercises on machine operation, and a pat on the back to achieve performance expectations. Another group of trainees learning the same information might require intensive, small group training with extra practice on those same machines, videotapes in three different languages, frequent testing, and be assigned peer coaches after small-group training has ended. Both groups move from point A to point B, but the approaches are quite different, because the groups are made up of *different* people who are required to meet the same performance expectations.

Analyze Trainee Characteristics

You need to know your trainees. Not necessarily on a personal basis, although that would give you greater insight, but you should know enough about them to make some critical training approach and content decisions. What's enough *"training audience"* information? Start with the basics.

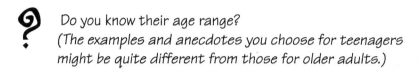

Do you know their age range?
(The examples and anecdotes you choose for teenagers might be quite different from those for older adults.)

Will your group be primarily male or female?
(If it's male, make sure your role plays aren't all centered on female characters.)

Do your trainees have a college education?
(Gauge test items and instruction level accordingly.)

See how important these considerations are? Keep going.

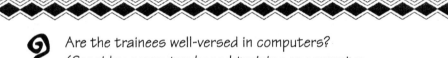

Are the trainees well-versed in computers?
(Consider computer-based training or computer exercises.)

Do they all speak the same language?
(If not, you'd better plan to split into bilingual groups, or assign or hire an interpreter.)

What are their reading abilities?
(You might not want to rely primarily on print material with lower-level readers.)

You get the point. The more time you invest in figuring out your trainees, the more effective your training will be. And, incidentally, the faster you'll be able to get your trainees from point A to point B.

Merilynne, Lionel, and Diane met ...

to discuss the employees who needed to be trained to make the linguine. *"I think all of the cooks should learn how to make the dough and operate the machines,"* Diane said. *"You really think so?"* asked Lionel. *"In my restaurant, only some of the cooks have been making the linguine. The others flip burgers and make the fries."*

"Then what do you do when your linguine makers call in sick and you can only get a burger flipper to fill in?" Diane asked. *"Good point,"* Lionel responded. *"I guess it's on my shoulders, or one of the other managers. Maybe all the cooks should learn."*

"Well," Merilynne interjected, *"whether or not you decide all the cooks should be trained, we can still get a pretty good picture of our trainees. Let's start listing things we know about them."* *"Like the fact that all of them are male?"* Lionel asked. *"Is that correct?"* Merilynne countered. *"In my restaurant, yes,"* Lionel said. *"I have one female cook,"* Diane said. *"But Lionel's right. Most of the cooks are male."* *"Let's list that on the flip chart, then,"* Merilynne suggested. Together the team came up with more general characteristics to describe the trainees.

✔ Primarily male audience

✔ approximately 75% part-time employees

✔ approximately 50% high-school students, 25% college students, 25% grammar-level education

✔ approximately 40% Hispanic (*varied from 0% at some locations to nearly 85% at others*)

✔ varying levels of technical experience and language levels

✔ varying levels of reading ability

Complete A Trainee Demographics Matrix

The following trainee demographics matrix is a tool you can use to analyze your trainees. It will start you thinking about how you can select the most appropriate training strategies for your trainees. Add or delete categories to fit your particular situation. For example, maybe you don't need to know your trainees' math skills, because those skills aren't required for job performance. On the other hand, perhaps you could use the following: information regarding skills your trainees may/may not have mastered, reason(s) for attending training, cultural mix, interests, any entry-level skills already learned, and so forth.

TRAINEE DEMOGRAPHICS MATRIX						
Organization/Division: _____						
Training Program: _____						
Trainee Group	Demographics					
	Education	Math Skills	Language Skills	Age	Motivation	Historical Data

The historical-data column refers to any information that affects training design preferences, including methods to avoid. For example:

- ❖ Will there be many distractions for this group of trainees (e.g., phone calls, interruptions to take care of "business," etc.)? Make sure that expectations are agreed upon up-front regarding interruptions.

- ❖ You may have employees who feel pressured to get "real" work done as training proceeds and may start showing up late, taking extended breaks, etc. You need to be sensitive to this while reinforcing the need for training.

- ❖ Will your group include fast learners? Make sure you design extra, more complex exercises for fast learners, and prepare to team them as mentors with slower learners. You don't want them getting bored or "tuning out."

- ❖ Will computer learning be included? Then avoid online demonstrations that don't have trainees keying in information along with the trainer.

- ❖ Are your trainees geared toward hands-on activities (many are), or are they theoretical thinkers who like to ponder possibilities?

- ❖ Will your group include those who have an aversion to writing? If you need responses from them, provide tape recorders so they can tape their responses or elect scribes to capture key points.

- ❖ Will your trainees learn better if you spread training over a couple of weeks or months, or will it work to their benefit to conduct a comprehensive weekend session?

The tainee demographics matrix will help you get a good grip on your target audience—the employees who will participate in the training. If you understand your trainees, and the content you're covering, you're closer to choosing a training approach that will fit them.

Consider Training Approaches

 The characteristics of your trainees will influence your choice of a training approach as much as any other consideration. As well they should. After all, it's for them. But just in case you'd like some other input that might sway your choice, consider the following tips.

Recall what's worked for you in the past

Maybe you or someone in your organization has a great repertoire of ideas to help your training situation. If they've proven successful, use them. Maybe you have a couple of fun icebreakers, or you've designed a great peer-training program that far exceeds what's out there. If it will work to help your trainees fulfill their training objectives, don't hesitate to use it.

Think about your resources

Money isn't the only resource to consider here, although it may influence your choice. If the money's tight, don't bother considering expensive videotapes or renting a room in a fancy hotel for your training. On the other hand, don't lavishly spend money where it won't help. Keep your objectives and goals firmly entrenched in your mind, and be creative.

 Other resources you might think about include employees who could lend a hand in translating materials into a different language, any video or audio equipment your organization has *(or that other employees have and might be willing to lend)*, community rooms for rent *(at minimal cost)*, and so forth. Be limited only by your creativity.

Involve the trainees in your decision

Don't just consider your trainees. Get them involved from the beginning. Ask for their opinions. Encourage them to help you choose an approach. Don't be surprised if they suggest simpler, straightforward approaches rather than some of the more sophisticated methods available today.

Get to know your trainees, rely on what's worked before, consider your resources and involve your trainees in decisions regarding training approaches. Keep these steps in mind as you consider the group instruction, coaching/one-on-one, and self instructional training options in the next three chapters.

CHAPTER FIVE WORKSHEET:
CONSIDER YOUR TRAINEES

Fill out the following trainee demographics matrix for the trainees involved in a current training effort. Write in three appropriate categories in the demographic column heading boxes.

TRAINEE DEMOGRAPHICS MATRIX			
Organization/Division: _____ **Training Program:** _____			
Trainee Group	**Demographics**		

. List any successful training approaches you have used in the past that may work well for this situation.

---

2. List any resources that might be available to you for training development and delivery.

---

3. List the ways you can involve your trainees in choosing training aproaches.

GROUP INSTRUCTION OPTIONS

Are you considering *(or have you already decided)* to use group instruction? If so, you're in the majority. Group instruction is used more than any other method. It normally utilizes a wide variety of techniques such as lecture, large and small group discussion and problem solving, role plays, games, individual exercises and writing various responses and key points on flip charts.

You may decide to choose group instruction because it's more economical, and the diversity of opinions provides for energetic discussions and interesting role plays. Or you may have no choice but to instruct your trainees in a group setting.

If you have fifty employees to train, it may be difficult to train each individually. However, you may try to split the training audience into smaller groups of more manageable size.

Whatever the case may be, if you are training a group of employees, you'll have to work hard to incorporate trainee participation *(rather than just lecture)*.

Group instruction is typically effective for improving knowledge, attitude, and some skills. Your choice of materials and strategies often includes the use of video, participant workbooks, overhead transparencies, slides, detailed reference materials and computers where appropriate. If you would like an overview of some options you have available when you choose to train a group of employees, read this chapter. It will give you guidelines for planning.

Planning A Skill-Building Session

A skill-building session attempts to teach employees a skill you have identified in your training objectives. Showing and practicing the skill are the major components of this type of group session. It's your job to model the skill competently, and provide enough time for your trainees to master it.

Structure your skill-building session so that trainees first get an idea of why they are being taught this skill; then show them how to do it, provide sufficient practice time, and finally give them feedback. Basically, this session can be broken into three segments:

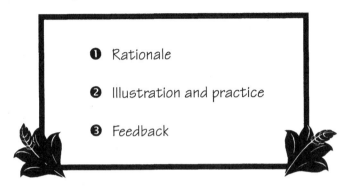

❶ Rationale

❷ Illustration and practice

❸ Feedback

Limit your time in the first segment. You want your trainees to know the importance of why they are being taught this skill *(and what's in it for them)*, but you don't want to drone on for hours. The main purpose of this stage is to motivate your trainees. Keep that in mind, put yourself in their place, and you'll keep it short.

The second segment is the meat of the skill-building session. First, show your trainees how to perform the skill the way you want them to perform it, and clearly explain your performance expectations in measurable terms. Answer questions and provide plenty of practice time. Of course, you need to provide whatever equipment your trainees need, and try to replicate the conditions in which your trainees will have to perform the skill.

The third segment involves feedback that you provide to the trainees regarding their performance during training, and the feedback you get from them regarding the skill they are developing. First, you need to check that they are performing the skill the way it should be performed. If they aren't, you'll intervene and help them succeed. Second, you need to solicit feedback from them concerning the skill. In what areas are they having difficulty? Do they have any ideas on how it should or could be done differently? Respond to their feedback and sum up the session.

Planning A Lecture

If you're training a large group, you'll most likely include a lecture or demonstration in your training session. It's typically low cost, and can accommodate a large number of people.

If you're attempting to impart knowledge and your trainees want to learn the information, a lecture can work well. But don't plan a dull presentation. The last thing you want to do is encourage your trainees to fall asleep!

How do you set up a lecture that is aimed at helping your trainees improve their performance? A key step is to know your trainees, so you're only covering information they don't know, and work at involving them in your lecture.

In the introduction, you have a limited amount of time to grasp the attention of your trainees. Bore them now, and you'll lose them. Start with an interesting fact, example, or story. Tell them what you're going to teach them, and be sure to add how it will help them. Motivate your trainees so they'll tune into your lecture!

Add visual aids to the body of your lecture when possible. It helps to illustrate each major point that you make. Use an overhead or computer screen projector, white board, flip charts, etc.

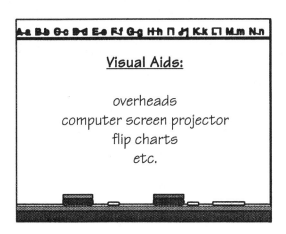

Visual Aids:

overheads
computer screen projector
flip charts
etc.

Again, be sure to use every possible opportunity to involve your audience. Ask the trainees for their input and comments throughout the lecture, provide plenty of examples that apply to your trainees, and set up a question-and-answer period.

Finally, in your conclusion, review the key points of your lecture and the major discussion points raised. End by motivating your trainees. If performance improvement is your goal, they should leave the lecture *wanting* to improve their performance and knowing how to go about it.

Preparing Case Studies And Role Plays

Case studies and role plays are sophisticated training techniques that require careful facilitation. They also involve more time and commitment on the part of both the trainer and the trainees. However, if your topic is complex, and there are many possible solutions or criteria, case studies and role plays can provide insight that less interactive techniques cannot.

Case studies

Case studies involve problem situations that need to be solved. You provide the trainees with enough background material to make a problem seem *"real"* and to allow the trainees to develop plausible solutions. You also give them several questions to ensure a specific outcome. You can either write the case study, or use video or audiotapes. Most case studies average about half a page, but some can be much longer.

Here's an example of a brief case study, relating to a training situation:

ADTECH, Inc. is a small, but rapidly expanding advertising agency of 25 employees *(and counting)*. New hires seem to pop-up weekly, making their small office space even more cramped, and everyone is having to double up on their workstations. All the while, business is booming and everyone has more projects than they can handle.

For the last few months, the weekly staff project review meetings have been anything but productive. Some people go off on tangents, some get vindictive, while others keep quiet and don't say anything. Plus, the leader uses the meetings to push his ideas and beliefs down the participants' throats. At times, no one can get a word in edgewise. Long-term employees want to go back to the way things *"used to be,"* and the new employees are tired of hearing about it.

In the past, the meetings went smoothly and ended in less than an hour. Now they can go more than two and a half hours and practically nothing gets resolved! Projects are beginning to suffer and clients are experiencing unacceptable delays. In addition, there is counterproductive talk going on in the halls and people are starting to take sides.

Clearly, they need help in order to work together. The president has decided to call on a training consultant to come in and work with the group. There has been some resistance to this because the group feels that they don't need anyone "from the outside" telling them what to do. You're the training consultant. How will you proceed?

Have trainees respond individually, either verbally or in writing, or respond as a group in a discussion. Use a case study if you can make it realistic, if your details allow your trainees to develop useful solutions, and if you can debrief it successfully in the time allotted.

Role plays

A role play can be a supplement to a case study. In such an extended case study, the problem or solution is acted out rather than described. Trainees who play roles are given descriptions, while the rest of the audience is given a guide that tells what they should be looking for during the role play.

A role play can also be an improvisation. In the improvisation, trainees play themselves but try out new behaviors to test them out. For example, a trainee may be asked to deal sympathetically with a hostile customer. The trainee, then, will try to be as sympathetic as possible. The trainee is given a brief amount of information and the audience receives a detailed worksheet for observation.

What role are you playing?

Here's an example of a role description for a trainee who's playing a customer phoning into a service center.

You are an executive for a small financial services firm and find that you are traveling most days out of the month. All of this travel is making you spend more late nights in the office (*when you're there!*) finishing up all the work that you can't do on the road. A business associate you respect has a notebook computer and is able to do her work on airplanes and at other "*downtimes.*" Just think of it, no more late nights!

Since business is going well, you have been given the "*OK*" to purchase a notebook computer. You are calling a computer manufacturer's customer service department to find out more information about this computer and its compatibility with your office's current system. You also need to know where you can get one because you're ready to buy.

Essentially, you are calling to get more information on a specific notebook computer, the "*xyz-123 portable.*" You want to know that it is compatible with your system, and you don't want to go to a lot of trouble or waste a lot of time to find the right one.

You are a results and action-oriented person, without a lot of patience for details. People who get bogged down and can't see the forest for the trees frustrate you, since they seem to focus on holding things up rather than getting things done. Especially frustrating are people who beat around the bush and ask a whole lot of needless questions—why don't they "*just do it?*"

If the Service Representative asks a lot of peripheral questions and doesn't recognize your style and "*urgency,*" quickly and abruptly focus the discussion.

Here's an example of a role play observations worksheet. Observers can check categories and make notes regarding areas they want to discuss after the role play.

TELEPHONE AND INTERPERSONAL SKILLS	Role Play Observations Role Play #: _____ Service Rep: _____
5 STEP TELEPHONE INTERACTION PROCESS	
Connect	❑ Develop your "Quality Service Attitude" ❑ Set the stage
Gather	❑ Listen actively ❑ Overcome barriers to communication
Decide	❑ Analyze and decide ❑ Follow through
Reply	❑ Respond to customer's request ❑ Clarify and verify the information
Close	❑ Summarize the key points ❑ Thank the caller
3 KEY INTERPERSONAL SKILLS CATEGORIES	
Attitude	❑ Project professionalism ❑ Demonstrate empathy ❑ Show enthusiasm ❑ Be service-oriented
Behaviors	❑ Listen actively ❑ Remain objective/flexible ❑ Offer alternatives ❑ Communicate constantly ❑ Accept personal accountability
Voice & Language	❑ Choose language carefully ❑ Avoid jargon ❑ Use vocal variety
STRENGTHS:	
AREAS FOR IMPROVEMENT:	

A discussion should always follow a role play to ensure that the trainees have a chance to provide comments and insight. The most important learning often takes place in the discussion phase of a role play.

If trainees take the role play situation seriously, and you debrief it well, role playing can successfully encourage transfer of training. It brings trainees closer to real-life situations, and actively involves them in the learning process.

If you think that case studies and role plays are appropriate for your training situation, you may even consider having your trainees combine the two. Have trainees look over the case study, then ask specific individuals to develop certain characters and role play them. Afterwards, follow through with a discussion.

Group instruction is both challenging and rewarding. If you plan your sessions well, incorporate a wide variety of activities that involve your trainees, and seek to improve performance as described in your training objectives, your approach will succeed.

CHAPTER SIX WORKSHEET:
CHOOSING GROUP INSTRUCTON OPTIONS

1. Briefly describe the ways you're currently providing trainees feedback on their performance during a skill-building session. Note how you might improve your feedback methods.

_____

_____

_____

2. Describe one or two techniques you might use to enliven your training lectures.

_____

_____

_____

3. Briefly describe an idea for a case study or role play you might create for an upcoming training session.

_____

_____

_____

COACHING/ ONE-ON-ONE OPTIONS

Although you might associate training with a facilitator who motivates and trains a group of individuals, some of the most effective training occurs with just two people—a *"coach"* and an employee. In fact, if you consider yourself a non-trainer, many of your training experiences will be one-on-one.

Do consider one-on-one training seriously. It has great potential for being highly successful, but you must plan carefully and focus on your objectives *(sound familiar?)*.

On-The-Job Training

If you are being asked to train another individual on the job, you have the advantage of targeting your training toward a particular person who will benefit from the individualized instruction. Get to know your trainee and her particular background skills, knowledge, likes, dislikes, and motivating factors, and you'll have the edge when it comes to training.

Likes
Dislikes
Skills
Knowledge

Most on-the-job training consists of teaching specific skills. So, you'll follow the same preparation steps for a skill-building session as outlined in the previous chapter. For example, you'll tell your trainee why he is being taught a particular skill, you will show him how to do it, you'll let him practice it, and you'll give and receive feedback.

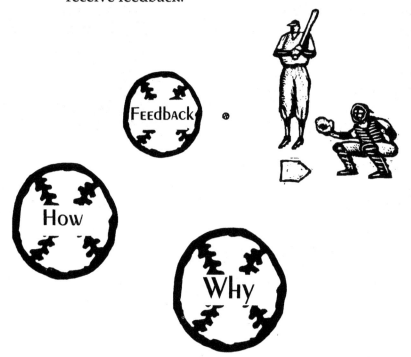

Of course, one-on-one coaching typically takes more time than group training sessions, yet the approach has many advantages. You can focus on motivational techniques that will inspire your particular trainee, not a group of diverse individuals. As you model the skill, you can answer specific questions more elaborately, without worrying about other trainee knowledge, skill, or interest levels. You can closely observe your trainee practicing the skill and provide immediate feedback, and your trainee can share her observations right away. You can reenact this scenario until all the new skills are learned. Because you're probably working together you'll be in contact after the training, and you can offer appropriate rewards on a continuing basis.

Mentoring

You may be asked to mentor another individual, which is actually like long-term one-on-one training. A mentor provides a role similar to an expert craftsman watching over the development of an apprentice. It involves a careful description of what skills, knowledge, and attitudes the employee needs to learn and develop, and a plan for achieving those goals.

If you are chosen as a mentor, you must conduct a needs analysis to determine the need for and the scope of training, including performance expectations. Mentoring usually involves the following steps:

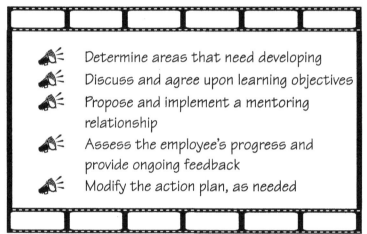

Determine areas that need developing

Discuss and agree upon learning objectives

Propose and implement a mentoring relationship

Assess the employee's progress and provide ongoing feedback

Modify the action plan, as needed

If your assessment, training, measurement, and follow-through of the employee emulate the steps in the High-IMPACT Training Model, your success as a mentor will be unparalleled. But your success also depends on the support you receive from your organization.

If your organization considers mentoring a worthwhile and necessary activity (*it is supported and rewarded*) and it is written into job descriptions as a performance expectation, mentoring can become one of your organization's greatest developmental strengths.

Peer Training

You may simply not have enough time to train or coach all of your employees. Perhaps one-on-one training would be best in your situation, but you couldn't possibly sit down with each of the twenty employees in your department and spend the necessary time for them to master new skills. You could, however, train two or three adept employees how to effectively train and coach their peers.

You may have to give up some of your management responsibilities and control in the process, but it could lead to increased motivation in your peer trainers, and save you time and money.

Don't make your peer trainer decisions immediately without careful consideration. Often your first thought of who might make a great peer trainer isn't the best. You want someone outgoing, but also patient. You need good performers, but only if they can explain directions well. Choose employees whom you hold in high esteem. They should have excellent work values, be respected by their peers, and represent your organization well. Their attitudes are critical, since they will be role models for the peers they train. Remember, some employees would rather not be peer trainers, so you should not coerce anyone into this position.

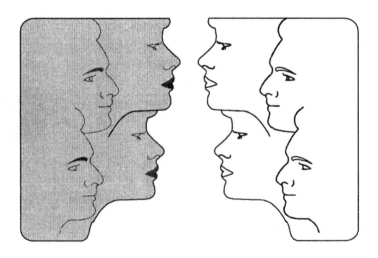

Once you have chosen your peer trainer(s), you'll have to instruct them on how to go about the training experience. If they already possess the knowledge, skills, or attitudes you want them to impart, discuss how they can best transfer those attributes to their peers. Share this guidebook with them!

Each peer trainer should have a training plan for each lesson. Make sure that your peer trainer knows:

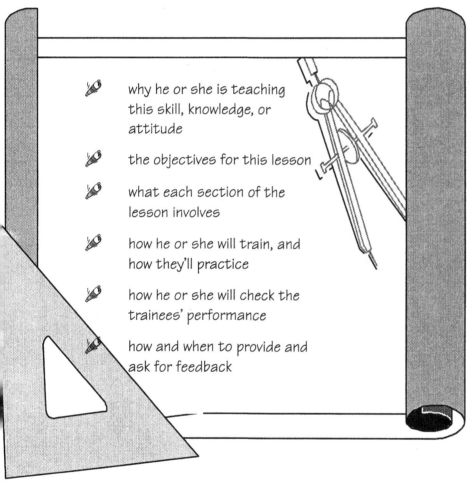

- why he or she is teaching this skill, knowledge, or attitude

- the objectives for this lesson

- what each section of the lesson involves

- how he or she will train, and how they'll practice

- how he or she will check the trainees' performance

- how and when to provide and ask for feedback

The training plan need only be a brief summary that lists the information above. You can also provide a separate sheet on which to list each trainee's progress.

Arrange frequent contact with the peer trainer to identify what works, what needs modification, and how the training is going. Your job as trainer isn't completely replaced. You still have to supervise the process and step in as needed. But the payoff can be particularly rewarding, especially for peer trainers who enjoy helping others improve their performance. And remember, peer trainers should have the training aspect of their jobs included in their performance and reward plans.

One-on-one training can be your ticket to individual performance improvement. Whether it involves on-the-job training, mentoring, or peer trainers, employees benefit from the new learning challenges, and your organization benefits from employees who are being taught to perform to its expectations. It's a win-win situation!

CHAPTER SEVEN WORKSHEET: YOUR ONE-ON-ONE OPTIONS

.. Consider one of the Coaching/One-On-One options covered in this chapter, and list the reason(s) why such an approach may be appropriate for one of the current or future training needs in your organization.

_____

_____

_____

_____

_____

_____

_____

_____

_____

_____

_____

_____

_____

_____

SELF-INSTRUCTIONAL OPTIONS

When is a self-instructional approach appropriate? If your trainees are similar in many attributes, except for certain knowledge and/ or ability to learn at the same pace, self-instruction may suit them better than group instruction. If you have employees who can't be taught in a group situation *(perhaps you need them on the job, and they require small, flexible time slots for training)* consider self-instruction. If you can't teach all of your trainees in central locations *(maybe they're located at franchises around the country or world)*, self-instruction may be an excellent option for successful training.

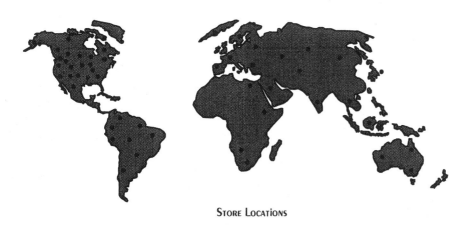

STORE LOCATIONS

Whatever your decision, you'll find it helpful to look at some of the *"self-instructional"* options available.

Correspondence Courses

Correspondence courses usually take place via mail, with the trainer located at a distance from his or her trainees. To set up a successful correspondence course, you have to write clearly defined lessons accompanied by application exercises and test questions where appropriate. Your tests must be able to clearly measure the trainee's accomplishment of the course objectives.

Correspondence courses can work well. Some of the conditions for success are:

⊡ The content is primarily knowledge-based.

⊡ Your trainees can work independently.

⊡ The training content doesn't necessarily depend on human interaction (e.g., your trainees aren't learning how to become counselors).

⊡ Training can be spread over a period of time.

⊡ Your trainees strongly desire to meet the course objectives.

⊡ Your trainees get something out of the course (e.g., a degree, reward, promotion, etc.).

⊡ You are motivated to oversee your trainees' success.

Computer-Based Training

Modern technology has brought us a number of new self-instructional methods, including computer-based training, interactive video, and multi-media.

If you have access to these technologies for training *(which we'll refer to as "CBT" in this section),* keep the following tips in mind.

Some of the same stipulations for correspondence courses apply to CBT. You need employees who can pace themselves, and who are willing and able to complete a self-instructional program.

CBT requires learners who are comfortable with computers and who can get their hands on one. Easy access is the key. If it takes too much trouble to complete the program, you will cut your success rate. Also, keep in mind that face-to-face instructional methods might be better for training employees to become better sales people, or to increase their interpersonal communication skills.

If your trainees have the above prerequisites for CBT, the advantages are many. They include the following:

- Learning can be individualized by allowing trainees to complete the course at their own pace, and to enter at various levels.

- CBT often provides both immediate and continual feedback. Trainees don't have to wait for a trainer to validate their performance.

- Since trainees have to respond to computer prompts, CBT provides an active (as opposed to a passive) learning situation.

- CBT directs trainees toward competent performance and doesn't end until trainees have achieved it.

- CBT can train individuals in less time.

- Since trainees can pace their own learning, the training situation may be less stressful and of more interest.

- CBT allows for accurate tracking of each trainee's learning.

- Trainers have more time to help individual trainees.

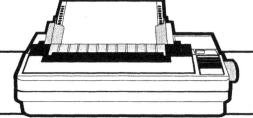

Although the advantages are numerous, disadvantages also exist. Some trainees don't like computers, or they may not have the motivation to complete a self-paced program. If not enough computers are available, training may take too long too complete. CBT can also be expensive and time consuming to develop and update. Designing a computer-based course is demanding and requires specific skills.

Ask yourself the following questions about any CBT course you are interested in implementing:

1. Will it allow the trainees to fulfill all of your training objectives?

2. Does the course incorporate enough practice exercises to ensure transfer of learning?

3. Does it use the most appropriate learning strategies to teach the specific attitudes, skills, and knowledge?

4. Do you have the resources to develop (or purchase) and manage CBT?

If your organization has the resources to develop or purchase CBT, and you can manage the process effectively, consider it.

Whole-Course Projects

A whole-course project isn't an addition to training; it *is* the training. It involves asking an individual to take on a task your organization considers important, in an attempt to stretch that individual's learning potential.

The trainee in this case isn't just practicing what she has learned. She will learn by doing what she is asked to. For example, you might ask a manager to head a team tasked with identifying and providing solutions for workflow process problems. Your purpose depends on your trainee's skills. She's either already competent as a team leader but needs to learn how to identify problems and propose solutions, or she's skilled in problem solving but needs training in leadership. You focus on one area.

Usually, the best candidate for this type of training is a professional who qualifies for it, and has the capacity and the desire to learn and grow professionally. He should also have assistance if needed, so don't dump a heavy assignment on him and then disappear. Provide learning resources such as books, videotapes, and self-instructional programs for reference if necessary. Supervise, but do so discreetly. The key here is to learn through a real-life experience, rather than train for it beforehand.

Job Aids

Is training absolutely necessary? Or will a well-designed job aid do the trick? A job aid is a tool usually written, illustrated, or online (*such as "Electronic Performance Support Systems"*) that provides instruction and reference. Have you ever bought an answering machine with the instructions printed on a sticker that is taped to the

machine? That printed sticker is the equivalent of a job aid. Instead of reading through the manual and trying to recall the instructions, you only have to look at the sticker and read a concise version of the directions.

To listen to messages, press:
1. Rewind, then
2. Play

Job aids reduce the need for recalling knowledge or skills. From a training perspective, that means instruction may not be needed. Sometimes, however, job aids are created in tandem with instructional materials, thus reducing the need for extended training. They may be considered a self-instructional option, because they are an alternative or adjunct to training that you can use on an individual basis.

Job aids are typically less costly to develop than instruction, can be created more quickly, and can be revised easier. You may not recall some of the ten steps to satisfying a customer if you attended a training session a while ago, but it's hard to ignore the ten steps if they are posted in your workstation.

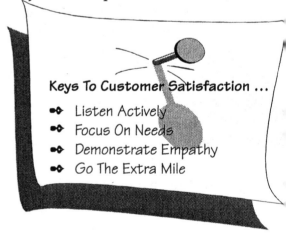

Keys To Customer Satisfaction ...
● Listen Actively
● Focus On Needs
● Demonstrate Empathy
● Go The Extra Mile

Use job aids when:

- **the skill is difficult to master**
  (e.g., a new computer program requires certain commands that aren't easy to recall)

- **the task is cumbersome**
  (e.g., managers are asked to review procedures based on several different criteria)

- **the skill or task is rarely performed**
  (e.g., financial analysts prepare a cost/benefit analysis annually)

- **the skill or task is anticipated to change**
  (e.g., newly hired restaurant servers need to know food abbreviations for ordering from cooks, even though a new computer-automated system will go into effect in a few months)

- **time and money are limited**
  (e.g., sales clerks hired for the Christmas rush need to learn to operate the cash registers)

In these situations, job aids will benefit an organization and its employees. If you are in doubt as to whether job aids should replace or supplement your training effort, ask yourself these two questions:

"Will a job aid satisfy the training objectives?"
"Can I add job aids to training in order to increase performance?"

If your answer to at least one of the questions is *"yes,"* don't hesitate. Create a worthwhile job aid and get feedback from your employees on how it improves performance.

Merilynne, Lionel, and Diane ...

considered the use of job aids for the cooks at Country Kitchens. *"I'm not sure job aids should replace the training sessions,"* Merilynne said. *"The cooks need the hands-on training and practice to learn to make dough that is up to our standards. No job aid can simulate what the dough should feel like. The right texture comes with practice."*

"But wouldn't a job aid help as a reminder of the amounts of ingredients?" Diane asked. Lionel nodded, then added, *"And a job aid would definitely come in handy for operating the machine. It's a step-by-step procedure."*

"You're both right," Merilynne commented. *"All cooks need the hands-on training, but job aids posted in the cooking station might help to ensure success. Especially since most of the cooks are part-time workers and the turnover rate is pretty high."* *"But don't forget,"* Diane added, *"that the job aids need to be written in both English and Spanish. Otherwise, they won't be one hundred percent effective."* The team continued discussing how they should create the job aids.

The self-instructional options presented in this chapter run the gauntlet from being inexpensive and fairly easy to produce to costly and challenging to create. Each option has its own advantages and disadvantages. Weigh each and determine which options best suit your situation.

CHAPTER EIGHT WORKSHEET:
YOUR SELF-INSTRUCTIONAL OPTIONS

Consider one of the Self-Instructional options covered in this chapter, and list the reason(s) why it may be appropriate for one of the current or future training needs in your organization.

_____

_____

_____

_____

_____

_____

_____

_____

_____

_____

_____

_____

_____

_____

DESIGN THE TRAINING

Choosing the right training approach requires as much focus as your efforts on performance goals, trainee considerations, and training objectives. You wouldn't choose your goals and objectives with care and discrimination, only to close your eyes, point to one of the training approaches listed in this guidebook, and say, *"This is it! We're going to use this one."* That would be comparable to renting a limousine for the gardener who heads to the neighborhood deli in search of grass seed. The vehicle doesn't fit either the passenger or the destination!

You need to choose your training approach with the same care and consideration you used to choose your goals and objectives. Your performance objectives will be achieved by your trainees if *(and only if)* your training facilitates the learning and mastering of the attitudes, skills, and knowledge required for achieving those objectives.

Consider The Elements Of Training Approaches

Before you can delve into designing your training approach, it's helpful if you know the basic elements of every training program. From there, you can tailor your approach to the needs of your trainees. Every training approach should include the following elements for successful transfer of learning.

1. Content information:

Why?

What?

How?

What do your trainees need to know? Every training approach involves some sort of content that describes *"why,"* *"what,"* and *"how"* the subject matter relates to customer requirements, the trainees, and/or the organization.

2. Training support materials:

Training support materials are the *"vehicle"* for conveying the content information covered during training. They can include printed, video, or online material, and should be developed carefully enough to be understood by the trainees without a lot of trainer support and/or discussion activity.

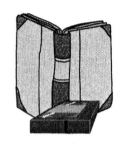

3. Exercises/testing (pre, during, and post):

You'll need to incorporate selected learning, practicing, and testing methods *(e.g., case studies, skill application, discussions, problem solving, etc.)*. The exercises are designed to help trainees learn, apply, and/or assimilate the subject matter during training, simulating the *"real world"* work environment as closely as possible. Testing will help you check to see if trainees have picked up on the subject matter.

4. Tools/job aids:

Include items that will help trainees apply and remember what they've learned. Use checklists, forms, quick-reference cards, or worksheets that trainees may use back on the job following training. Design them for easy application and be sure to incorporate key information from the training. *Producing High-Impact Learning Tools*, the next guidebook in the training series, details how to design these.

Different people learn differently, so try to incorporate as many different modes as you can, regardless of whether you're using self-instructional, one-on-one, or group training approaches. Appeal to visual learners with bright charts and innovative videotapes. Add experience-oriented exercises to grasp the interest of the learner. Include audiotapes, job aids, printed materials, observations, games, or whatever will give your trainees the extra edge to reach their performance goals.

What To Include

What content do you include in your training program? What practice exercises, if any, should you formulate? If this section has you concerned, follow this path …

 Look over each of your objectives. What content would be considered "must" include? Nice to include? Don't really need to include? Give it a good, honest look.

 Decide what type of practice your trainees may need to achieve each objective. For example, if one of your objectives is to increase the typing speed of your order-entry clerks to 60 wpm with less than 1% errors, provide them with computers on which to practice typing and give them plenty of time to practice.

Reconsider your trainees. Look back over your trainee demographics matrix, and write down what your trainees already do *(e.g., they currently type an average of 40 wpm with four to five errors per order)*. Will the content and practice you're considering move them quickly toward their performance goal? Or, could it be that additional, after-hours practice will help them achieve the objective, without new content training?

These considerations may help you eliminate some unnecessary instruction. It will hold you to your objectives and keep you from including unimportant things. You'll learn to use your time wisely by weeding out what won't lead to performance improvement, and including content you might have missed.

You'll also discover that you will alter your training methods based on whether you're teaching your trainees to improve attitudes, skills, or knowledge *(or a combination thereof)*. If you're trying to improve attitudes, you'll rely on lots of media and discussions. If it is skill improvement you're after, you'll provide tons of practice time. And if knowledge improvement is your goal, you'll most likely choose to drill and test.

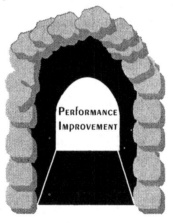

Create An Instructional Blueprint

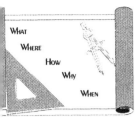

A key step in organizing any training effort is creating an instructional *"blueprint"* document. The blueprint will provide you with a detailed description of the *"what, where, how, why, and when"* of your project, including the development *and* delivery of training.

Training Approach Guidelines

Prior to developing your blueprint, you may want to consider some basic guidelines regarding training approaches.

Keeping in mind the information you've gathered regarding performance goals, training objectives, and trainee characteristics, consider the following *"generally accepted"* guidelines. Remember, there are exceptions to these rules of thumb, so consider your unique circumstances carefully.

	LEGEND
3 = Very appropriate	
2 = May be appropriate	
1 = Typically inappropriate	

		ATTITUDE	SKILLS	KNOWLEDGE
Group Instruction	Skill Building	1	3	2
	Lecture	2	1	3
	Role Plays	2	3	2
Coaching One-On-One	On-The-Job	2	3	2
	Mentoring	3	3	2
	Peer Training	1	3	1
Self-Instruction	Correspondence Courses	1	2	3
	Computer Based Training (CBT)	2	2	3
	Whole-Course	1	2	1
	Job Aids	1	3	2

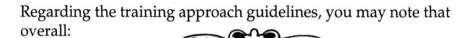

Regarding the training approach guidelines, you may note that overall:

> Mentoring is an effective method for training several areas (in fact, coaching/one-on-one options are very effective overall).
>
> Many different methods facilitate skill development.
>
> Few methods are appropriate for influencing attitude.

What To Include In An Instructional Blueprint

Creating a blueprint document is not necessarily a complex process. Regardless of how you organize or format the document, make sure you include the following components:

1. A *"big picture"* description of the training, including a general overview of expected performance improvement. This is your executive summary or *"elevator speech"* regarding the project.

2. Specific performance objectives in measurable terms.

3. Description of trainee audience(s) and important considerations.

4. Training approaches to be used to help trainees achieve performance goals (such as role plays, CBT, lecture, etc.).

5. Detailed content outline (or reference to a separate document that contains the content).

6. Description of *"deliverables"* (all materials and services to be produced or delivered, e.g., Trainer's Guide, Train-The-Trainer Sessions, videotape, etc.)

7. Resources (human, materials, tools, etc.) required to complete the project, and their associated costs.

8. A schedule for development, delivery, and evaluation.

You can see how important it is to create a blueprint. Without it, you'll be like a sailor without a ship, or a destination!

Planning The Order Of Training

You can't teach your trainees everything they need to know at once. Nor can you practice every skill simultaneously. Somehow you have to organize what you're going to do when. Is there a logical order to the skills or knowledge you're trying to teach your trainees? If so, follow it. For example, if you're training a group of sewing-machine salespeople how to thread a particular machine, you would start at the beginning *(with the thread spool)*, and continue through the steps until you finish threading the needle.

In other cases, the skills you teach may not have to be taught in order. If that's your case, you may choose to move from simple to complex, frequent to infrequent, or highest to lowest priority. In any circumstance, you'll need to combine all of your decisions regarding instructional approaches into a carefully organized plan.

Develop A Training "Map" or Plan

All training developers need an instructional "map," or plan for their training programs based on the instructional blueprint. It's one of the elements of every training program regardless of whether you're using Group, One-On-One, or Self-Instructional approaches. When you create a session plan, you describe an instructional *"process"* to achieve one or more of your training objectives. To create a training plan, you must:

> Organize general information
> Identify your content and training techniques
> Choose your resources
> Allocate a time for each section

Here's an easy-to-use template for training planning *(the techniques for completing it are explained on the following pages):*

Training Plan:_____

Program title:

Session/module: **Total time:**

Objective(s):_____

_____

_____

Visual aids/materials:_____

Time	Resources	Techniques / Content

. Fill in General Information

Complete the information at the top of the worksheet, including the type of training *(such as group instruction,* ne-on-one, or self-instructional; *write this on the blank line next to* 'Training Plan").

. Identify Your Content And Training Techniques

What do your trainees really need to know? List these things in detail, per the objectives and content you included n your blueprint. In this step of creating a training plan, you have to pare your content down to the core of necessity. You may be tempted to present information that would be beneficial to your trainees, but isn't necessary for them to reach their performance goals. If you have extra time, add this information. Otherwise, curb that urge!

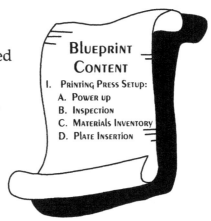

BLUEPRINT
CONTENT
I. PRINTING PRESS SETUP:
   A. POWER UP
   B. INSPECTION
   C. MATERIALS INVENTORY
   D. PLATE INSERTION

Can you arrange your content in a logical and/or chronological order? If not, try to create common groupings of information. Move carefully from what your trainees know to what they don't know, and ensure that they understand each step before you move on.

For each point or step you've detailed in your *"content plan,"* choose a training technique that will illustrate it. Will you be explaining? Demonstrating? Facilitating? Will questioning your trainees fit the situation? Decide which training technique will be appropriate, then write it down.

Choose your resources

List the resources you'll need to teach your trainees. Do you need a training room or a self-instructional resource center? What about work materials/tools, computers, an overhead projector, a television and VCR, a flip chart, and some markers? If you need it, list it in your plan. Then you won't forget it.

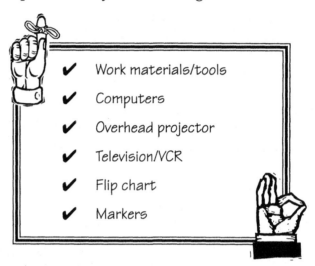

- ✔ Work materials/tools
- ✔ Computers
- ✔ Overhead projector
- ✔ Television/VCR
- ✔ Flip chart
- ✔ Markers

Allocate a time for each section

How long will each section take? Start with zero, determine how much time each section of your session will take, then note the cumulative time total next to each item. For example, you'll write *"5 minutes"* by the introduction. For a brief icebreaker, maybe you'll show a short video. The video is eight minutes long, so you write *"13 minutes"* next to the video. Then you're planning to deliver a 10-minute lecture to briefly explain a problem for discussion. Write *"23 minutes"* next to that portion of the lecture.

When you complete your training plan, you'll have a good idea of how long the session should take you. If your estimation coincides with the time you have allocated for the training, you're set. If your estimation is two hours and the training can only be 45-minutes long, you've got some serious cutting to do.

Merilynne, Lionel, and Diane referred ...

to their list of attitudes, skills and knowledge needed to make perfect linguine. Making the dough, operating the pasta machine, and cooking the sauce all needed to be mastered, but the order of training didn't appear critical. *"Besides, we don't have to train the cooks how to cook the sauce,"* Diane observed. *"They already know how to do that. It's a simple case of opening the sauce packet, adding it to the clams, and heating thoroughly. That's not a problem."*
"Which shall we start with then?" Lionel asked. *"I'd choose making the dough,"* Diane said. *"It's more hands-on, working with the flour, and much more fun in a training situation than working a machine."* *"I'll second that,"* Lionel agreed.

Merilynne, Diane, and Lionel came up with a training plan to teach the cooks how to make pasta dough correctly. Here is a portion of their Plan:

Training Plan: Group Training

Program title: In Search of Perfect Linguini with Clam Sauce

Session/Module: Making Dough   **Total time:**   45 minutes

Objective(s):   1. Decipher all abbreviations in linguine recipe

2. Read recipe and follow each step in order.

3. Mix dough for 3 minutes and verify that texture meets standards.

Visual aids/materials: Flip chart, markers, mixing cups/spoons,

flour, water, eggs, completed linguine (gooey, tough and perfect)

Time	Resources	Techniques / Content
10 Min.	Finished product	Facilitate: Introductions/objectives Experience: Let trainees taste samples
		Ask: Which sample tastes best?
		Explain: 1. Good dough makes good linguini; result = satisfied customers, profits. 2. Bad dough makes bad linguini; result = dissatisfied customers and lost $.
13 Min.	Cups, spoons	Hand out: mixing cups, spoons

Whether you're planning a skill-building session, a lecture, a case study or a role play, you'll need to create a training plan. It keeps you focused on your objectives and the time trainees need to complete objectives during training.

Measuring The Success Of Your Trainees

Why do trainers test their trainees? To see if training actually translates to performance. Your tests, then, should reveal a measurable difference in what trainees know, what skills they can perform, and how they feel or act. Develop test items that are closely tied to your objectives. Just as you don't want to include meaningless information in the content of your training sessions, don't add worthless questions to your tests.

Look at your objectives again. *(You should know them inside-out by now.)* Then write a test item that asks trainees to perform. Make sure the conditions in which you want your trainees to perform are present *(if possible)* in the test situation. For example, ask your order-entry clerks to type in sample orders that are identical *(or very close to)* orders they'll complete on-the-job. If the rooms in which they type are generally noisy, simulate those conditions and make sure the tools they use during training are the same or similar to actual job equipment.

You may want to steer away from written tests, especially if you are checking skill levels. Your tests should be performance-based when possible. For example, the order-entry clerks may  be able to tell you where all the keys on the computer board are located, but unless they can actually type 60 wpm with less than 1% errors in an actual situation, they haven't fulfilled the objective and reached your performance expectations.

A group of new employees may be able to list all of the safety considerations you taught them, but you need to see if they will follow them in an actual situation. Likewise, the salespeople you are training may be able to tell you how to deal positively with customers, but unless you simulate a situation or watch them interact with actual customers, you can't gauge how much of their learning has translated into improved performance.

"If we want the cooks to ...

be able to decode abbreviations, can't we just give them a test with various abbreviations and ask them to write them out?" Lionel asked. *"You'd know that they could interpret the abbreviations,"* Merilynne said, *"but would you know that they could pick up a measuring cup and measure the flour exactly as the recipe asked?"* *"I see what you're trying to say,"* Lionel said. *"Why quibble over whether they can write it? See if they can actually do what we want them to."*

"Exactly," responded Merilynne. *"Besides, if you gave the cooks a written exam, they might not do well because of language differences, or reading ability, or writing skills. You want them to take a recipe and follow the directions exactly. So ask them to do that."...*

Practice After The Sessions Are Over

Are there any instances where you would want training practice to continue after the initial training sessions have ended? Certainly, if the situation allows for it. Then trainees can apply what they've learned in training to a real-life situation. An added benefit is that it enhances the learning that has taken place.

For example, you might give managers who have just completed a training course on problem solving a *"practice"* project to identify problems in their departments and provide ideas for solutions. Once the project was complete, the trainer could meet with the manager to provide some feedback and coaching based on the manager's performance.

Just about any training approach that you design should include content information, training support materials, exercises and/or test items, and tools or job aids. You'll base your choice of these items on your particular objectives and trainees in order to tailor

the approach until it fits like a glove. Then, once you've created your instructional blueprint and training map, you're ready to develop and pilot test your program.

CHAPTER NINE WORKSHEET:
TRANSLATING YOUR OBJECTIVES
INTO TRAINING

. Choose one of your objectives where post-training practice would be appropriate. Then complete each item:

Objective:

_____

_____

_____

_____

_____

A. Briefly outline the major content item(s) you need to teach to achieve this objective *(in the appropriate order)*.

_____

_____

_____

_____

_____

B. What type of practice will your trainees need to achieve this objective?

_____

_____

_____

_____

_____

_____

_____

C. Write a test item for this objective.

_____

_____

_____

_____

_____

_____

_____

_____

2. Create the first page of a training plan for one of your training projects.

Training Plan:_____

Program title:

Session/module: **Total time:**

Objective(s):_____

_____

_____

Visual aids/materials:_____

Time	Resources	Techniques / Content

PILOT TESTING AND IMPROVING YOUR TRAINING

It all looks great on paper. Your training objectives support your goals, and your training approach is custom-made for your group of trainees. Everything should go off without a hitch. Well, maybe. Or maybe not. How will you know if your training plan is on target if you don't try it out?

Conducting A Pilot Test

Training, like a Broadway show, requires rehearsals. Would you fly with a pilot who spent a great deal of time preparing and working out the details of his first transatlantic flight, but had never actually flown it before? Pilot testing is your chance to get the bugs out of your training effort. It's a quality check.

Conduct your pilot test by trying out either the separate components you have prepared, the whole training effort, or both.

Consider the following tips:

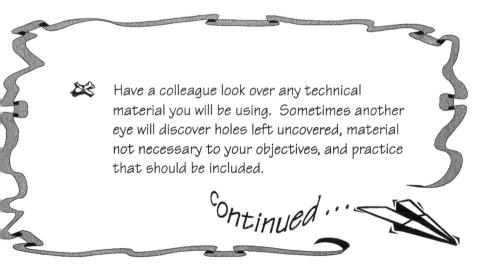

Have a colleague look over any technical material you will be using. Sometimes another eye will discover holes left uncovered, material not necessary to your objectives, and practice that should be included.

Continued...

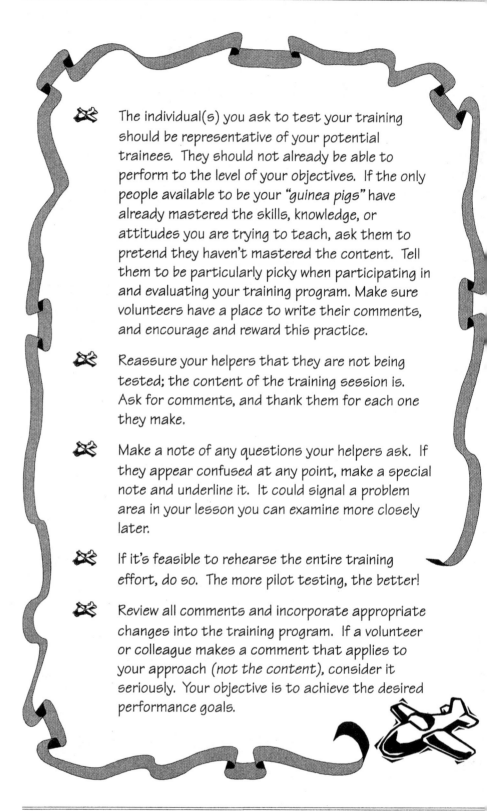

The individual(s) you ask to test your training should be representative of your potential trainees. They should not already be able to perform to the level of your objectives. If the only people available to be your "guinea pigs" have already mastered the skills, knowledge, or attitudes you are trying to teach, ask them to pretend they haven't mastered the content. Tell them to be particularly picky when participating in and evaluating your training program. Make sure volunteers have a place to write their comments, and encourage and reward this practice.

Reassure your helpers that they are not being tested; the content of the training session is. Ask for comments, and thank them for each one they make.

Make a note of any questions your helpers ask. If they appear confused at any point, make a special note and underline it. It could signal a problem area in your lesson you can examine more closely later.

If it's feasible to rehearse the entire training effort, do so. The more pilot testing, the better!

Review all comments and incorporate appropriate changes into the training program. If a volunteer or colleague makes a comment that applies to your approach (*not the content*), consider it seriously. Your objective is to achieve the desired performance goals.

Working Toward Improvement

Your pilot test should provide you with critical information. You will learn whether:

(a)   your training will accomplish your objectives;

(b)   your training needs some critical revisions; or

(c)   you need to rethink your training effort and start over.

Answer *"a"* doesn't necessarily mean that your training is perfect. It could be the pilot testing identified some areas of improvement (*e.g., the video you chose was nothing to write home about, or the computers seemed a little slow*), but changing those areas isn't keeping your trainees from fulfilling the training objectives. What, or who can't use improvement? Your quest is to continuously improve your training efforts.

Did the training accomplish its objectives?

This is the do-or-die test. If your training doesn't accomplish the objectives you set for your trainees, it definitely needs improvement. You'll have to find out where it falls short. If ninety percent of the trainees can fulfill the objectives, do some detective work to uncover why the ten percent don't get it. Is it just one objective that's beyond their reach? Maybe you need to provide additional practice on that skill.

If you have ensured that your objectives are measurable, this task will be much easier. Then, you can identify whether trainees have fulfilled the objectives; if they haven't, you'll know to what degree they've bridged the performance gap, and you can improve your program accordingly.

Improvement potential

If you're interested in upping the success rate of your training effort, consider the following improvement tips.

➥ Work on the most important improvements first (e.g., the ones that have the biggest impact on your most important objectives).

➥ Gain momentum by starting to make improvements, any improvements! Your success will encourage you to make other changes that will improve your training effort.

➥ Work on improving what you can do yourself, without having to get the okay from others in your organization. For example, improve your job aids by adding illustrations, if that's an improvement you can do by yourself.

Finally, list all additional potential improvements. Think about:

➥ providing a more comprehensive, convincing rationale for learning.

➥ ensuring that trainees fully understand the objectives, and specific performance expectations.

➥ providing a superior learning environment (minimal distractions, positive feedback, quality training resources, plenty of practice time, etc.).

➥ enhancing your explanations, examples, job aids, etc. to facilitate learning.

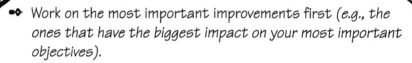

Merilynne, Diane, and Lionel decided …

to pilot test their training on Nigel Christensen, the owner of Country Kitchens, and five of the cashiers at the restaurant Lionel managed. *"Nigel may not fit the trainees' description exactly,"* Merilynne commented, *"but he doesn't know how to make the linguine or operate the pasta machine. The cashiers fit the mold pretty well. Two are Spanish-speaking, all are part-time, and one hasn't completed high school. All in all, they should provide us with some valid feedback."*

The pilot test provided results that came close to what they expected. All of the volunteers learned how to make the dough and operate the machine. But the sessions took much longer than they had anticipated and the bilingual approach didn't work very well. *"It's good we figured this out during the pilot test,"* Diane said. *"I think we should split the English and Spanish speakers into two groups and train them separately."* *"I agree,"* Lionel said. *"Then the sessions can be completed in the time we allotted."*

Tackle the improvements that will help your trainees bridge the performance gap and increase their value to your organization.

Pilot testing isn't just an option if you take your training effort seriously … it's a mandate! Its purpose is to help you see your training in a different light—that is, from your trainees' perspective. In so doing, you step back and open the door for improvement. It's an opportunity you can't afford to pass up.

CHAPTER TEN WORKSHEET:
THE PILOT TESTING PROCESS

1. List the key steps you would use to plan and implement a pilot test for an upcoming training program in your organization.

_____

_____

_____

_____

_____

_____

_____

_____

_____

_____

_____

_____

_____

.. List five key considerations for evaluating and improving a training program.

1. _____

_____

_____

2. _____

_____

3. _____

_____

_____

4. _____

_____

_____

5. _____

_____

_____

CHAPTER ELEVEN

SUMMARY

When you map your training approach, you travel quite a distance. It takes you from the tail end of a needs analysis and comes to a halt just before you produce your learning tools. In between those two destinations is territory that prepares you for the road ahead. The twists and turns, the potential pitfalls, and the roadblocks challenge you to focus on the journey in front of you.

First, you have to decide what performance improvements your employees need to make. The turns will be easy to maneuver if the performance goals you set are linked to corporate goals and are both descriptive and measurable.

Second, you have to create training objectives that support the performance goals. This step in the journey can throw you a curve. You have to prove that training will help your employees bridge the performance gap, and you have to write training objectives that clearly state the expected performance.

Third, you have to carefully study your potential trainees and consider their unique characteristics prior to choosing a training approach.

Fourth, you will work on designing your training. All training requires certain elements, just as all vehicles require fuel, wheels, an engine, etc. The design of those elements, however, will differ depending on your choice of training. Group training is uniquely different from one-on-one or self-instructional learning. Likewise, a 4-wheel drive truck is designed differently and covers rough terrain better than a Ford Pinto. Your training should be constructed to move your trainees comfortably and securely toward success, and pilot testing will help you reach that goal.

If you have mapped your training approach well, you'll be able to begin training with your journey planned, your vehicle wisely chosen, and your destination certain. It's a far better way to go!

REPRODUCIBLE FORMS AND WORKSHEETS

The pages in the Appendix are provided for you to photocopy and use appropriately.

TRAINEE DEMOGRAPHICS MATRIX						
Organization/Division: _____						
Training Program: _____						
Trainee Group	**Demographics**					

SAMPLE ROLE PLAY
OBSERVATION SHEET

TELEPHONE AND INTERPERSONAL SKILLS	Role Play Observations Role Play #: _____ Service Rep: _____
5 STEP TELEPHONE INTERACTION PROCESS	
Connect	❏ Develop your "Quality Service Attitude" ❏ Set the stage
Gather	❏ Listen actively ❏ Overcome barriers to communication
Decide	❏ Analyze and decide ❏ Follow through
Reply	❏ Respond to customer's request ❏ Clarify and verify the information
Close	❏ Summarize the key points ❏ Thank the caller
3 KEY INTERPERSONAL SKILLS CATEGORIES	
Attitude	❏ Project professionalism ❏ Demonstrate empathy ❏ Show enthusiasm ❏ Be service-oriented
Behaviors	❏ Listen actively ❏ Remain objective/flexible ❏ Offer alternatives ❏ Communicate constantly ❏ Accept personal accountability
Voice & Language	❏ Choose language carefully ❏ Avoid jargon ❏ Use vocal variety

STRENGTHS:

AREAS FOR IMPROVEMENT:

TRAINING APPROACH GUIDELINES

		ATTITUDE	SKILLS	KNOWLEDGE
Group Instruction	Skill Building	1	3	2
	Lecture	2	1	3
	Role Plays	2	3	2
Coaching One-On-One	On-The-Job	2	3	2
	Mentoring	3	3	2
	Peer Training	1	3	1
Self-Instruction	Correspondence Courses	1	2	3
	Computer Based Training (CBT)	2	2	3
	Whole-Course	1	2	1
	Job Aids	1	3	2

WHAT TO INCLUDE IN AN INSTRUCTIONAL BLUEPRINT

1. A *"big picture"* description of the training, including a general overview of expected performance improvement. This is your executive summary or *"elevator speech"* regarding the project.

2. Specific performance objectives in measurable terms.

3. Description of trainee audience(s) and important considerations.

4. Training approaches to be used to help trainees achieve performance goals (such as role plays, CBT, lecture, etc.).

5. Detailed content outline (or reference to a separate document which contains the content).

6. Description of *"deliverables"* (all materials and services to be produced or delivered, e.g., Trainer's Guide, Train-The-Trainer Sessions, video tape, etc.)

7. Resources (human, materials, tools, etc.) required to complete the project, and their associated costs.

8. A schedule for development, delivery, and evaluation.

TRAINING PLAN
WORKSHEET

Training Plan:_____

Program title: _____

Session/module: _____ Total time:_____

Objective(s):_____

_____

_____

Visual aids/materials: _____

Time	Resources	Techniques / Content

Professional And Personal Development Publications From Richard Chang Associates, In

Designed to support continuous learning, these highly targeted, integrated collections f
Richard Chang Associates, Inc. (RCA) help individuals and organizations acquire the k
and skills needed to succeed in today's ever-changing workplace. Titles are available th
RCA, Jossey-Bass, Inc., fine bookstores, and distributors internationally.

Practical Guidebook Collection

Quality Improvement Series

Continuous Process Improvement
Continuous Improvement Tools, Volume 1
Continuous Improvement Tools, Volume 2
Step-By-Step Problem Solving
Meetings That Work!
Improving Through Benchmarking
Succeeding As A Self-Managed Team
Measuring Organizational Improvement Impact
Process Reengineering In Action
Satisfying Internal Customers First!

Management Skills Series

Interviewing And Selecting High Performers
On-The-Job Orientation And Training
Coaching Through Effective Feedback
Expanding Leadership Impact
Mastering Change Management
Re-Creating Teams During Transitions
Planning Successful Employee Performance
Coaching For Peak Employee Performance
Evaluating Employee Performance

High Performance Team Serie

Success Through Teamwork
Building A Dynamic Team
Measuring Team Performance
Team Decision-Making Techniques

High-Impact Training Series

Creating High-Impact Training
Identifying Targeted Training Nee
Mapping A Winning Training App
Producing High-Impact Learning 1
Applying Successful Training Tech
Measuring The Impact Of Training
Make Your Training Results Last

Workplace Diversity Series

Capitalizing On Workplace Diversi
Successful Staffing In A Diverse Wo
Team Building For Diverse Work G
Communicating In A Diverse Work
Tools For Valuing Diversity

Personal Growth And Development Collection

Managing Your Career in a Changing Workplace
Unlocking Your Career Potential
Marketing Yourself and Your Career
Making Career Transitions
Memory Tips For The Forgetful

101 Stupid Things Collection

101 Stupid Things Trainers Do To Sabotage Success
101 Stupid Things Supervisors Do To Sabotage Success
101 Stupid Things Employees Do To Sabotage Success
101 Stupid Things Salespeople Do To Sabotage Success
101 Stupid Things Business Travelers Do To Sabotage Success

ABOUT RICHARD CHANG ASSOCIATES, INC.

hang Associates, Inc. (RCA) is a multi-disciplinary organizational performance
ent firm. Since 1987, RCA has provided private and public sector clients around the
n the experience, expertise, and resources needed to build capability in such critical
rocess improvement, management development, project management, team
ce, performance measurement, and facilitator training. RCA's comprehensive package
, products, and publications reflect the firm's commitment to practical, innovative
s and to the achievement of significant, measurable results.

ESOURCES OPTIMIZE ORGANIZATIONAL PERFORMANCE

ING — Using a broad range of skills, knowledge, and tools, RCA consultants assist
developing and implementing a wide range of performance improvement initiatives.

— Practical, "real world" training programs are designed with a "take initiative"
Options include off-the-shelf programs, customized programs, and public
e seminars.

LUM AND MATERIALS DEVELOPMENT — A cost-effective and flexible alternative to
affing, RCA can custom-develop and/or customize content to meet both organizational
and specific program needs.

RODUCTION — RCA's award-winning, custom video productions provide employees
mation in a consistent manner that achieves lasting impact.

IONS — The comprehensive and practical collection of publications from RCA supports
onal training initiatives and self-directed learning.

D PROGRAMS — Designed for first-time and experienced trainers alike, these programs
prehensive, integrated materials (including selected Practical Guidebooks) that provide a
e of flexible training options. Choose from:

s That Work! ToolPAK™
-Step Problem Solving ToolKIT™
ous Process Improvement
d Training Program

- Continuous Improvement Tools, Volume 1 ToolPAK™
- Continuous Improvement Tools, Volume 2 ToolPAK™
- High Involvement Teamwork™
  Packaged Training Program

RICHARD
CHANG
ASSOCIATES

World Class Resources. World Class Results.^{SM}

Chang Associates, Inc.

Headquarters
on Parkway, Suite 300, Irvine, California 92618 USA
-8096 • (949) 727-7477 • Fax: (949) 727-7007
fo@rca4results.com • www.richardchangassociates.com

ices in Irvine and Atlanta • Licensees and Distributors Worldwide